Welcome to North America

by Mary Lindeen

Table of Contents

Meet the Neighbors.................2

Canada 4

Mexico......................7

The United States 10

Sharing the Land 13

Glossary....................15

Index 16

Consultant:
Adria F. Klein, Ph.D.
California State University, San Bernardino

capstone
classroom

Heinemann Raintree • Red Brick Learning
division of Capstone

Meet the Neighbors

North America is the third largest **continent** on Earth. This huge land area is freezing cold in the north, and warm and tropical in the south. In between are mountains, plains, deserts, cities, farms, and millions of people.

North America is home to Canada, Mexico, and the United States. Each of these countries is different from the other, even though they are right next to each other. Let's take a tour of these North American neighbors.

Canada

Canada is the second largest country in the world. It is at the top of North America. Forests cover much of Canada. There are also mountain ranges and clear blue lakes. Bears, wolves, and moose all live in the Canadian woodlands.

The **capital** city of Canada is Ottawa. It is a busy city with many museums. Visitors to Ottawa and other parts of Canada will hear people speaking French and English. Both are the national languages of Canada.

In 1867, people from northern regions of North America joined together to become one nation, called Canada. Every year on July 1, Canada Day is celebrated in honor of this event. People enjoy picnics, parades, and fireworks. They also wear the red and white colors of their flag.

Mexico

Mexico is in the southern part of North America. It is warmer here. There are deserts and wet tropical rain forests. There are mountains and farms. People from all around the world travel to Mexico to enjoy its warm sandy beaches.

The capital city is Mexico City, one
of the biggest and oldest cities in
the world. The city is a popular
gathering place for **residents** and
visitors.

A big celebration occurs in Mexico on Cinco de Mayo. That means May 5th in Spanish, the **official** language of Mexico. In 1862, Mexican soldiers won an important battle against the French. Today people dance, sing, and eat traditional foods on Cinco de Mayo.

The United States

The United States is between Canada and Mexico. Like both of those countries, it has many different natural areas. There are deserts, mountains, forests, and beaches. Alligators swim in rivers and swamps. Mountain lions like this one live on rocky cliffs.

Fifty states make up the United States. Most Americans speak English. The capital city is Washington, D.C. It was named after George Washington, the first president of the United States. Visitors come to see the city's old buildings, national monuments, and museums.

Marching bands like this one are common in the United States on the Fourth of July. So are picnics, fireworks, and flags. That's when Americans celebrate the day they became an **independent** nation in 1776.

Sharing the Land

Other island nations are part of North America as well. Greenland, the largest island in the world, is one of these countries. Each island country has its own **identity** including holidays, symbols, and flags.

Together, the countries of North America share mountain ranges, rivers, and oceans. They share borders and many parts of their past. North America is one land that is shared by many countries and many people.

Glossary

capital   the city where people in a country's government work

continent   large land mass made up of different countries

identity   who you are; the set of features that makes someone or something who they are

independent   free from the control of other people or things

official   approved by someone in authority

resident   a person who lives in a particular place

Index

capital. 5, 8, 11

Canada, 3–6, 10

Canada Day, 6

Cinco de Mayo, 9

flag, 6, 12, 13

Fourth of July, 12

Greenland, 13

language, 5, 9, 11

Mexico, 3, 7–9, 10

Mexico City, 8

Ottawa, 5

United States, 3, 10

Washington, D.C., 11–12